DIVING TO THE PAST

DIVING
TO THE PAST

Recovering Ancient Wrecks

W. JOHN HACKWELL

CHARLES SCRIBNER'S SONS / NEW YORK

ACKNOWLEDGMENTS

The author wishes to acknowledge the gracious assistance of Patrick Baker, staff photographer with the West Australian Maritime Museum, and that of his wife, Yvonne, who worked tirelessly in researching this project.

Charles Scribner's Sons Books for Young Readers
Macmillan Publishing Company, 866 Third Avenue, New York, NY 10022
Collier Macmillan Canada, Inc.

Printed in Japan
Book design by Vikki Sheatsley

First Edition   10   9   8   7   6   5   4   3   2   1

Library of Congress Cataloging-in-Publication Data
Hackwell, W. John   Diving to the past.
    Includes index.
    Summary: Explores the field of marine archaeology, describing how scientists locate, explore, excavate, and preserve ancient shipwrecks, the dangers involved, and the historical and cultural significance of such finds.
    1. Underwater archaeology—Juvenile literature.   2. Shipwrecks—Juvenile literature.
[1. Underwater archaeology.   2. Shipwrecks.   3. Archaeology]   I. Title.
CC77.U5H32   1988   930.1′028′04   87-233529   ISBN 0-684-18918-6

To the memory of my father, Richard Neville Hackwell, whose encouragement and financial assistance enabled me to attend art school at a very early age. Good friends are friends forever.

CONTENTS

Treasure
under the Sea

● ● ● Inscriptions from the Ancient Near East reveal that mankind has been fascinated by the sea since the beginning of time. Indeed, the myths of the Sumerian peoples, dating from the third century B.C., contain tales involving the mysterious powers of the deep. The Biblical writers, in their stories of creation, the flood, and Jonah's entombment in the whale's belly, echo the earlier Sumerian tales.

The ancient peoples also had a very practical connection to the sea. As early as 4500 B.C. the inhabitants of Mesopotamia dived for the murex shell to obtain a purple dye for use in royal garments, and less than one thousand years later the Egyptians searched the sea for mother-of-pearl, which they used to inlay funerary masks. By the time of the Phoenicians, who became the great maritime traders and merchants of antiquity, international shipping routes in the

Aegean, Mediterranean, and Red Seas were well established, and reports of shipwrecks with the loss of very rich cargoes led many divers to attempt recovery of sunken treasure.

For thousands of years, however, divers could remain underwater only two or three minutes at a time. (Sponge divers of ancient Greece and some modern Pacific Island inhabitants are legendary for their ability to remain below the surface for twenty minutes on one lungful of air, but these tales are quite fantastic.) Twentieth century technology has dramatically changed all that. The invention of the aqualung in 1943 by Frenchmen Jacques-Yves Cousteau and Emile Gagnan has accelerated the interest of the average person in the exploration of the oceans. Scuba diving is now such a popular family sport that centers and diving schools are located in almost every seacoast city in the world.

The invention of the underwater camera has given further impetus to interest in leisure diving. The world's first underwater photograph was taken in 1894 by Louis Boutan, also a Frenchman. Since those early beginnings spectacular refinements have enabled present divers to obtain magnificent photographic records of their encounters in the deep. In today's climate of concern for the environment and the preservation of delicate ecosystems, many people prefer to dive with a camera rather than with a spearfishing gun.

Modern leisure diving has resulted in the chance discovery of many shipwrecks. Fascination with undersea treasure is often so intense that teams of amateurs may hack at a submerged hull to break off a brass porthole, for instance, often with little regard for the historical context of the sunken vessel and without reporting the wreck to the appropriate authorities.

In the western world deep-sea diving is viewed as a glamorous exercise, with all the thrills of modern high risk adventure. There are frequent stories of shark attacks, competition for loot among participants, and conflicts over the division of sunken treasure.

The great majority of divers, however, act

Retrieving huge objects, such as this iron cannon, requires well coordinated recovery efforts. Once the tie ropes and airlift bags have been secured, most of the divers leave the water and return to the support vessel. Here a lone diver guides the cannon to the surface.

These Spanish "pieces of eight," displayed with a ship's bell, remind the viewer of the spectacular and valuable cargo that was carried on early galleons.

responsibly, and it is to such people, as well as to many fishermen and beachcombers, that marine archaeology owes gratitude. Divers and beachcombers have sometimes reported a chance find to government authorities, while fishermen have reported that their trawl nets snagged on what they suspected was a submerged wreck. Such reports have led to major discoveries of cultural, historical, and archaeological significance.

Marine archaeology, also called nautical or maritime archaeology, is the discipline responsible for the systematic excavation and recovery of early ships wrecked at sea. Often sponsored by universities, governments, and concerned private donors, marine archaeologists seek to recover artifacts for public display. Of supreme importance are objects that relate directly to a nation's history of settlement and development—such as vessels dating from the seventeenth and eighteenth centuries in America and from the nineteenth in Australia.

All shipwrecks contain information con-

Many modern expeditions undertake associated environmental studies. Here marine biologists collect coral samples from the project area.

cerning trade and interaction between countries. They also help us to understand primitive equipment and practices on board various ships, thus becoming a link with the past.

Marine archaeology is a multifaceted discipline involving a number of sciences. When a wreck is discovered, surveyors are asked to locate and map the site, and marine biologists gather information on the immediate environment. Corrosion chemists, metallurgists, and engineers become involved with the recovery of cannons and other metal objects. Historians seek to discover the circumstances that led to the shipwreck. Computer experts write complex programs enabling them to produce three-dimensional graphics of the wreck area. Archaeologists, conservationists, and others try to coordinate a recovery project that may, for financial reasons, last for several years.

Since an ability to dive is not necessarily a prerequisite for membership in an expedition, professional scientists combine their skills with those of amateur divers who join the expedition as part of a volunteer dive squad. For this and other reasons marine archaeology has become an extension of modern leisure diving, thus making its results more accessible and of greater educational and cultural value to the peoples of the world.

Dangers of the Deep

2

●●● Marine archaeology is fraught with its own special dangers. Unfortunately for modern research, ancient mariners didn't sink their vessels in convenient locations. Many wrecks are resting in almost total blackness some two to three hundred meters (650 to 1000 feet) below the surface. In such settings huge swells prevent a supply vessel from anchoring above the site. In rough seas excavation ships, which have been virtually transformed into floating archaeological laboratories, are forced to completely shut down until calmer weather permits the operation to continue.

Other wrecks are to be found in more shallow waters, perhaps on jagged coral reefs. While diving visibility may be enhanced by the shallow location, sudden tidal surges can sweep a diver long distances from the support vessel.

When diving to sunken wrecks, marine archaeologists face some very serious hazards. Divers may plunge enthusiastically below the surface only to find themselves among a large number of tiger sharks or bronze whalers. The worst danger to the diver, however, relates directly to the aqualung.

When divers have spent twenty minutes at depths of fifty or more meters (160 feet) breathing compressed air, they must surface very slowly to give their bloodstream time to clear. When divers descend to even greater depths they need to make regular decompression stops as they return, remaining stationary for up to fifteen minutes or more. If a diver fails to observe this precaution, air in the bloodstream forms into tiny bubbles that virtually burst when the diver nears the surface.

Even worse than failing to rest at selected intervals is the failure to exhale on ascent. A diver who is panicked by the presence of a hostile shark, for instance, may hold his or her breath while attempting to escape to the surface. This is the worst mistake, and it brings the worst consequence—death—through an air embolism, an explosion of the lungs.

Nitrogen narcosis is a disease very common among divers. Its symptoms are drowsiness and dizzy feelings that result from extended periods underwater. For this reason dive times are always regulated to enable divers to maintain peak fitness throughout the excavation.

Apart from some special dangers at sea, the lifestyle of marine archaeologists is similar to that of the more well-known land-based archaeologists.

While marine archaeologists tell stories of shark attacks and the dangers of air embolism, their land-based counterparts point out that they confront scorpions, spiders, and venomous snakes, sometimes returning to their freshly dug trenches only to discover that a nasty snake has claimed the new hole as its home.

Looters are a common annoyance in both fields of archaeology. Desperate divers have been known to use excessive explosive charges to obtain treasure from a sunken wreck where systematic multidisciplinary excavation work

Divers fall into the ocean over the side of an inflatable rubber raft. Such rafts are used by marine archaeologists when shallow water prevents the entry of larger vessels.

is in progress. Such irresponsibility totally despoils the underwater site. These divers are like the looters and grave robbers who for centuries have successfully plundered land-based archaeological sites all over the Middle East. Dig directors there have been known to pay local guards to patrol the excavation constantly, and some have even camped among the ruins for the duration of the dig.

Both land-based and marine archaeologists find that their respective environments have guaranteed the preservation of buried treasures. On land, the sands of time have swept over and buried ancient settlements. This sand, free of all moisture, preserves ancient artifacts and human remains for thousands of years. Indeed, if moisture was to contact any of the ruins, by way of an underground spring or other forms of seepage, many priceless objects would be lost.

On the other hand, salt water surrounds and preserves ancient shipwrecks. When a vessel settles on the seabed, vertical timbers may be broken off by shifting currents, but sand and other sediments settle about the hull while coral and crustaceans take hold of other portions, thus burying the ruins on the ocean floor. In this way, ship and treasure are preserved in wet sand. On the land, the absence of moisture preserves, while under the sea the opposite is true.

Yet another aspect common to the two fields of archaeology relates to the decay and loss of organic materials of historic value.

When Vesuvius erupted in A.D. 65 and destroyed the Greek city of Pompeii, molten lava buried animals and people alive. Such was the speed and ferocity of the destruction that many people were buried while they slept.

When systematic excavations began at Pompeii, archaeologists discovered that remains of humans and animals trapped in lava flow had completely decayed, leaving, in many cases, rooms littered with unusual lava cavities. Archaeologists found that by pouring plaster into these cavities they obtained exact replicas of the absent contents.

When the lava crusts had been chipped away, the remaining plaster casts provided an

Since many ancient wrecks have been buried for centuries in silt and mud on the ocean's floor, water dredges are used to clear the way for excavation and recovery.

incredibly accurate detail of the last moments of Pompeii. One cast was that of a dog, tied to a stake, unable to flee the lava. It died in a contortion of pain. In the city jail, many humans were found huddled together on the floor, attempting to shelter from the rushing lava flow.

In the same way, maritime archaeologists discover curiously shaped formations of coral and concretion among the ruins of a sunken wreck. Subsequent investigation reveals that these formations once contained an object that has completely vanished. Only a cavity remains. By retrieving the coral and pouring plaster or fiberglass resin into the cavity the archaeologist obtains a replica of a lost maritime artifact. Without this record all knowledge of the object would be lost. Such casts, whether originating from a land-based or deep sea excavation, make a vivid display in any museum.

While government support, funding, credibility, and recognition are vital to both fields of archaeology, marine archaeolgists are

A conservator examines a three-hundred-year-old broom made of twigs, called a besom. It may take two years of chemical baths before this artifact is available for public display.

A field conservator gently empties the contents of a ceramic jar in order to preserve any artifacts that may be trapped inside.

Salt water contamination is damaging to earthenware ceramics, and acids cannot be used to remove blemishes since they will cause further deterioration. Here a ceramicist uses polyvinyl acetate adhesive to join pieces of a broken jar.

quick to state that undersea excavation and recovery are much easier and preferable to work on hot dry land. Sand and mud surrounding a wreck on the ocean floor is not compacted like the mounds on the land that hide a buried city, and the sea itself is very useful to the archaeologist when it becomes necessary to remove the slimy mud.

When Howard Carter discovered Tut-Ank-Amun's tomb in Egypt in 1922, he employed hundreds of laborers who worked for several months to remove seventy thousand tons of sand and rubble that had covered the tomb entrance. If this had been an underwater project, four divers using huge water dredges could have completed the work in far less time.

While survey and excavation procedures are similar to both disciplines, undersea archaeology places unique demands on the director. On a land-based dig the director is free to spend many daylight hours participating in actual field work. There is sufficient time for informal conferences with the various specialists, and the director can be called immediately to assist at the scene of an important discovery.

At sea, however, a director, like all team

divers, can dive to the wreck no more than twice a day—and then only for a limited time. All excavation procedures are carefully rehearsed on board the dive ship, and the director must delegate authority to the divers on the ocean floor.

While the project director carries ultimate authority and responsibility for the success or failure of the work, in a diving expedition much emphasis is placed on decision-sharing since divers can't talk to one another when they are down at the wreck.

Born in an age of modern technology, facing unique challenges and special limitations, marine archaeology owes much of its success to the way it has adapted and made use of such technology. Indeed, the main difference between land-based excavation and undersea archaeology is perhaps the latter's overwhelming reliance on electronic gadgetry.

Searching for Lost Wrecks

3

● ● ● Early ships became wrecks for different reasons. First, storms blew some ships off course and they drifted dangerously until they either sank in the huge swells or foundered on rocks or reefs. Other ships lacked precise navigational instruments and charts, with the result that they became lost at sea. Many sailing ships sank as a direct result of gun battles on the high seas, while others, old and unseaworthy, were intentionally sunk. Most sunken wrecks ultimately served as shelters or breeding grounds for a complex variety of marine life.

The more remote the wreck is, the better preserved and undisturbed it is likely to be. The hostility and inaccessibility of the world's vast oceans have preserved valuable information on past

Artifacts recovered from a wreck often provide vital evidence relative to the ship's origin or last port of call.

eras. More than two thousand Spanish vessels, for example, were lost in the New World in just three hundred years, and the majority of those were in depths of less than thirty meters (100 feet). By 1830 an estimated five hundred ships were sunk annually in the Caribbean and along the east coast of North America, and that number increased dramatically during the Civil War.

It is naturally more difficult and time consuming to locate a wreck that is buried than one exposed on a beach or reef, but the results are likely to be more rewarding since turbulence caused by tides and disruptions caused by storms, so frequent along the coastline, are unable to buffet the sunken structures.

While some discoveries are the result of a chance sighting by fishermen or others on a recreational adventure, most are directly due to extensive searching by trained experts. Modern technological innovations have given rise to a variety of scientific search techniques, which, conducted in waters where ships were known to have been wrecked, pro-

duce satisfying results.

Aerial search involving low-flying spotter aircraft has occasionally been rewarded with sightings in shallow calm waters. If visibility is especially clear, large objects such as cannons, anchors, and hulls have been seen from the air in water as deep as fifty meters (160 feet).

The side scan sonar is a device used to detect ferrous objects—that is, those containing iron—on the seabed. It is towed on a cable at the rear of the search vessel and operates on the principle that echoes from various seabed features are picked up on the side of the trailing device, which in turn sends the echoes along the tow line to a special graphic recorder on the boat. The recorder transcribes the signals to a computer graphic to produce an acoustic image, which, to the trained eye, is as easy to interpret as a photograph. The side scan sonar has proved very successful in detecting nineteenth- and twentieth-century wrecks.

Since most ancient wrecks had no ferrous metal, search teams use a sonar device called

Computers are used to record dive times, crew fatigue, and individual tasks completed, as well as the usual graphic display of the total wreck site.

a sub-bottom profiler. This unit is similar to the side scan sonar, but in this case the signal is directed downward where it penetrates the sediment to produce a profile, or shadow graph, of any large buried object. The profiler's signal can easily penetrate three meters (ten feet) of mud or slime on the ocean's floor, making it a very useful search aid.

The cable sweep is another, far less costly, method. It is simply a cable suspended between two vessels and weighted to enable it to drag very close to the floor of the ocean. When the cable snags, a buoy is dropped and a diver is sent below to investigate. The cable sweep often reveals how much debris has been dumped into the oceans of the world.

When a buried object is confirmed as a wreck, a diver takes a magnetometer to the seabed to establish the perimeters of the sunken vessel. The device can be held in one hand and is simple to use. Any ferrous objects will change the undersea magnetic field and give a positive reading on the magnetometer. But again, its use is more successful with nineteenth- and twentieth-century remains.

At the conclusion of each search, marine archaeologists prepare a report for their controlling body or funding organization, in which they outline the search procedures they followed. If a wreck was positively identified, they outline its significance and the feasibility and cost of recovery. They also state the goals, limitations, and objectives of such an expedition and the time expected to bring it to fruition.

To ascertain the significance of a buried wreck is not an easy task. Obviously a wreck may contain artifacts of cultural value, but this in itself cannot justify the enormous expense of an undersea expedition. However, if the vessel is relevant to a particular historical event, then its recovery and preservation is of prime importance and often becomes a matter of urgency.

Before any decision to excavate is made, staff researchers, under the guidance of marine archaeologists, study historical records that may throw light on the wreck. Some-

A skilled diver guides a magnetometer along the boundary of the wreck area in an effort to detect any mass of ferrous metal hidden below the coral.

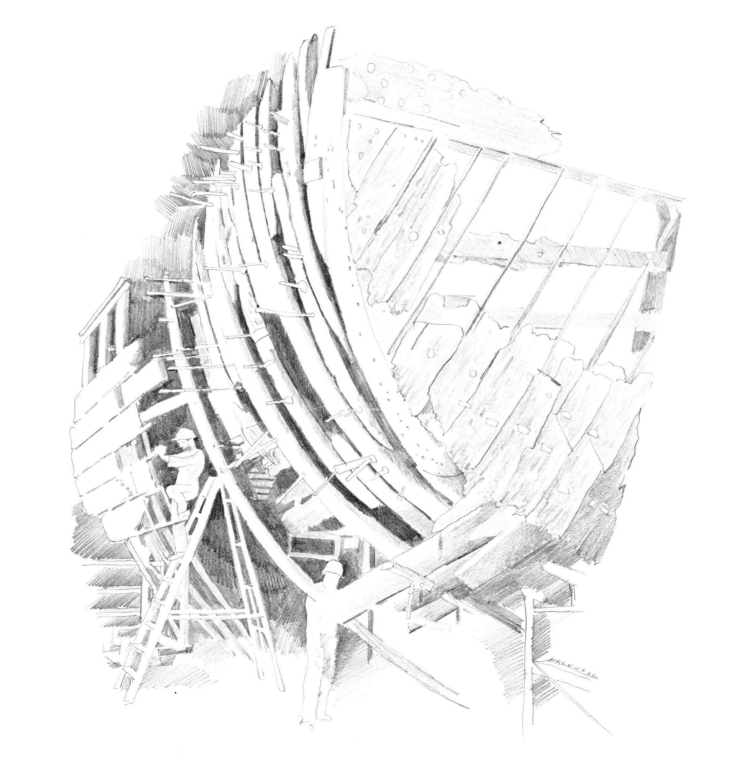

times a small dive team is sent to the area to conduct a preliminary survey.

If recovery becomes increasingly desirable, the team's administrative director sets about to complete a finely tuned estimate of the project. This estimate will be based on a number of factors, such as the accessibility of the wreck, the cost of renting a dive boat and equipment, and the number of staff needed, including their living expenses and salaries. Other more technical costs must also be assessed, such as the setting up of a field laboratory, a control and recording system, an environmental team, a survey and mapping room, and a photography laboratory.

Meanwhile, press releases are prepared in order to raise public awareness and increase the chances that private donors might fund the future expedition. It is also likely that a television network or popular journal will pay handsomely for the exclusive rights to report on the actual recovery project. All of this interest and support, together with the usual grants and direct government sponsorship, is marshaled in an effort to guarantee that the excavation and recovery take place within a few years of the initial sighting of the wreck.

Timber from an ancient vessel, fully restored after some years in special chemical wax tanks, is here assembled for public display.

The Dive Team

4

● ● ● The first scientific exploration of any wreck site generally takes the form of a predisturbance survey, test probe, and mapping and biological reconnaissance. This expedition lasts several weeks and may require two or three hundred dives, each of twenty minutes' duration.

Choosing the best dive boat is extremely important, and marine archaeologists consider that such a vessel must not only be super strong, it must be maneuverable, mechanically sound, and well equipped for the task. The dive boat will have stabilizers to keep the ship steady in rough seas and plenty of deck space to accommodate equipment and handle artifacts and pieces of wreckage. It must have lifting facilities and a large duckboard on the stern to make it easy for

Divers, resting on the duckboard of the recovery ship, offload a cache of coins and other artifacts that they recently collected at the wreck.

divers to enter and return from the water. Radar, depth finders for fixing over wrecks, auto pilot, generators, compressors, and such facilities as a computer room and photo laboratory are also considered standard equipment on any research ship. The crew and staff of the expedition need good accommodations and a recreation room for those long days when very rough weather produces turbulent seas and forces the postponement of all diving.

No long-term project can expect qualified staff and crew to return on future expeditions if the galley is not well stocked. Diving is physically demanding, and during the expedition the team will need a good supply of freshly baked bread, potatoes, fresh fruit, and vegetables. Such supplies can be brought to the boat if the wreck site is not too far from port. Some well-funded dives are so concerned for the long-term health and well-being of their divers that they take frequent electroencephalograms of the diver's brain response to the stress of deep sea exploration.

Even though members of the expedition may be called on to perform several roles, the excavation is divided into five broad categories: an archaeological team, a dive team, a biologial survey team, an on-board field laboratory team, and the ship's crew.

The marine archaeological team is headed by the project director, who is generally a qualified marine archaeologist. He or she directs the work of two or three field archaeologists, who in turn supervise their own dive teams.

The second working group is the dive team itself, and in this group the role of divemaster is of utmost importance. The divemaster must have a concern for the safety of the divers. He or she coordinates the dives and acts as a resource for information on tides, currents, and visibility. The divemaster plans the all-important decompression stops, giving consideration not only to the depth of the wreck but to the individual health and capacity of each diver.

The divemaster also must supervise the dive team's responsibilities when they are not diving, and since each dive lasts for only twenty minutes or so twice a day, the divers have plenty of time for such duties as refilling cylinders, collecting and labeling artifacts, and those extra tasks associated with dive equipment.

The divers themselves must be highly qualified people. They need to be expert at night diving, deep diving, diving with lights, navigation, and maintaining their own equipment such as air tank valves, regulators, and gauges. While it is hoped that they will not have to conduct an undersea rescue, divers must know how to perform a rescue under water and must know first aid procedures such as resuscitation.

Divers who apply to join such an expedition usually have had previous experience on an oil rig or other salvage operation. Some are also expert underwater photographers or explosives specialists whose skills are invaluable to the project.

The third working group is the biological survey team, and these members must also be good divers. This team is headed by a marine biologist and includes an underwater surveyor, who is expert at deep sea mapping.

The fourth group is the field laboratory team, as distinguished from the conservationists who work in permanent land-based laboratories and whose roles are considerably more permanent than those of the team on board the research vessel.

Directed by a corrosion chemist or a conservationist, the field laboratory team is responsible for the short-term preservation of

A diver relaxes after a strenuous period underwater. Here he demonstrates the use of the sextant.

large items and smaller artifacts of wood, leather, or various precious metals. Its job is to make sure that anything retrieved from the ocean's floor will not deteriorate while being taken back to the headquarters' laboratory.

The last group is the ship's crew. The captain of the ship heads this team, and he or she has ultimate responsibility for the safety of the crew and of the vessel. The crew includes an engineer, a cook, a physician, and two or three general staff.

Each day, the project director holds briefings with the head of each working team to ensure the smooth running of the dives.

Since most marine archaeological expeditions have a total of fewer than fifty people, opportunities are limited to those with the best qualifications—not just practical experience but academic achievements in marine studies. The participants must also guarantee that they intend to commit themselves to the duration of the project.

On the day before departure for the wreck

Working in almost total darkness, a marine archaeologist, carrying a rare and ancient navigational instrument called an astrolabe, returns to the waiting support ship.

On the right side concretions have almost obliterated the design on this beardman jug, but subsequent chemical baths reveal a jug of unusual beauty.

site, the team comes together for a period of orientation, which may include trial dives and final testing of new equipment. The project's core staff members explain to the team the working procedures and the goals of the expedition. Such briefings may last all day and include guest speakers participating in a seminar style series of lectures.

One of the special pieces of equipment certain to be demonstrated is the aluminum grid. The grid is a series of squares laid out and anchored over the wreck site, each square numbered to provide specific reference points. The grid is fundamental to the success of the ongoing exploration and is too complex to handle underwater without prior experience.

During the orientation period the staff becomes acquainted and learns to perform well together. Each member of the team speaks to the group and outlines his or her previous background and experience. At the end of the day expectations are high and the expedition is ready to begin.

While the search vessel anchors offshore, the excavation director instructs divers on how to assemble the prefabricated underwater grid.

Underwater Excavation Begins

5

● ● ● Once the vessel has anchored between the marker buoys that were previously laid out over the extremities of the wreck site, a professional photographer goes to the bottom to obtain predisturbance photographs of the entire wreck area. The photographs will have to be developed immediately to enable the director of the project to make preliminary assessments and to give instructions to the other working teams.

The photographer must meticulously plan his or her dives, for it is impossible to dive with a camera bag full of various lenses and several spare rolls of film. All details relative to visibility, lens selection, and format must be known before the dive.

A photogrammetist descends to the seabed with a specially designed underwater photo tower fitted with stereo cameras. From the pictures taken, a photomosaic of the entire site will be prepared.

Underwater camera equipment is very expensive. In addition to the camera itself, a photographer must have special waterproof housings and accessories, light meters and flash assemblies, as well as a wide range of film suitable for either natural light or artificial light.

The expedition director writes step-by-step instructions on a waterproof slate large enough for the photographer and associated divers to read on the seabed. The initial photographs utilize the photogrammetric technique—that is, a series of photographs will be taken in such a way that they can be linked together to form a mosaic or panorama of the whole wreck site.

Photomosaics often require the use of stereo cameras that can take highly detailed pictures of the contours. This is known as the planimetric view. While the photogrammetist is at work on the floor of the ocean, other divers, perhaps even the director, will check on the general condition of the wreck.

Once the photogrammetist has developed the film and assembled the photomosaic of the wreck, the survey specialists are ready to dive.

The next aspect of the expedition takes the surveyor and alternating dive teams several days to complete. The surveyor dives to establish a datum line above the wreck. It may measure fifty by twenty meters (160 by 65 feet), depending on the size of the hull. The surveyor uses either a theodolite or an electronic distance-measuring device, not only to obtain horizontal angles and measured distances but also to identify accurate longitudinal and latitudinal references. The surveyor also obtains detailed topographical features of the immediate geographical area.

The divers, working from the newly surveyed datum line, begin to lay the prefabricated grid until they have covered the area bounded by the survey. The grid is fixed into place by driving the vertical poles into the seabed and then attaching horizontal spacers between them, in order to prevent the vertical poles from moving about in cross-tidal surges.

The photogrammetist must assemble a series of photographs that match exactly the surveyed squares on the seabed. The photomosaic is then used by the director to instruct divers on procedures to be followed.

Each of the squares within the grid measures approximately ten by two meters (33 by 7 feet), depending on the system used, and is individually numbered to act as a landmark to orient the divers and to provide an accurate means of identifying the location of each artifact recovered. Without such knowledge an artifact would be merely a souvenir.

The grid further serves the information-gathering process because it permits the computer to produce three-dimensional graphics of the whole area. This information is especially valuable in understanding the placement of cargo and other such finds. If Italian goods, for instance, are discovered piled on top of English products, one can assume that the English cargo was the first to be taken on board the ship, since it was located lower in the ship's hold. From this information it is not difficult to postulate the ship's entry ports in order of sailings.

With the grid permanently in place, undersea mapping of the site begins. This is not a task for one lone diver since progress is very slow and often leads to painful frustrations.

All dive crews undertake to complete the mapping in rotation so motivation remains high and the results are achieved as soon as possible.

Each diver in the first team takes to the wreck a tape measure, waterproof pen, and matrix drawing board. They spend fifteen minutes or so suspended over a square, drawing all the features within that square. When it is time to resurface, they hand their equipment to the next team, who continues the process.

Underwater mapping is not a technically accurate process. A diver may drop the data in the course of his return to the surface, or the follow-up divers may not understand the map or may proceed to the wrong square altogether. The mapping process is helpful, however, in combination with the photogrammetric studies where the important areas can be redefined as the result of close-up mapping.

All divers, whether specialists or simply part of the support team, must carry some basic equipment on each dive: a knife for cut-

Using an amphibious theodolite, a surveyor obtains accurate horizontal angles and calculates distances on the seabed.

ting, scraping, or prising out small objects; a bag attached to the waist for carrying small finds to the boat; a stainless steel geologist's pick for breaking up crustaceans; a small buoy to mark newly observed objects for later attention.

If small artifacts are handy to the divers, even when covered in coral or other concretion, they can be easily retrieved and carried to the surface in a waist-bag. Objects cannot be safely carried by hand; they could be dropped and never seen again. Raising to the surface large objects, such as the portion of a hull or an anchor or a cannon, requires either a very substantial winch or air-lift bags tied to a sling or basket.

When it is time for heavy excavation, the divers take to the wreck a powerful water dredge that is served by a compressor on the supply vessel. This is strictly a calm water operation.

The dredge is like a giant suction cleaner capable of clearing away tons of mud, silt, and

This diver has anchored himself within a portable mapping grid. The drawing is secured to the grid while he uses a waterproof pen to draw a seabed plan on the tracing film that is masked to the board.

A small ivory carved knife handle recovered from an ancient wreck.

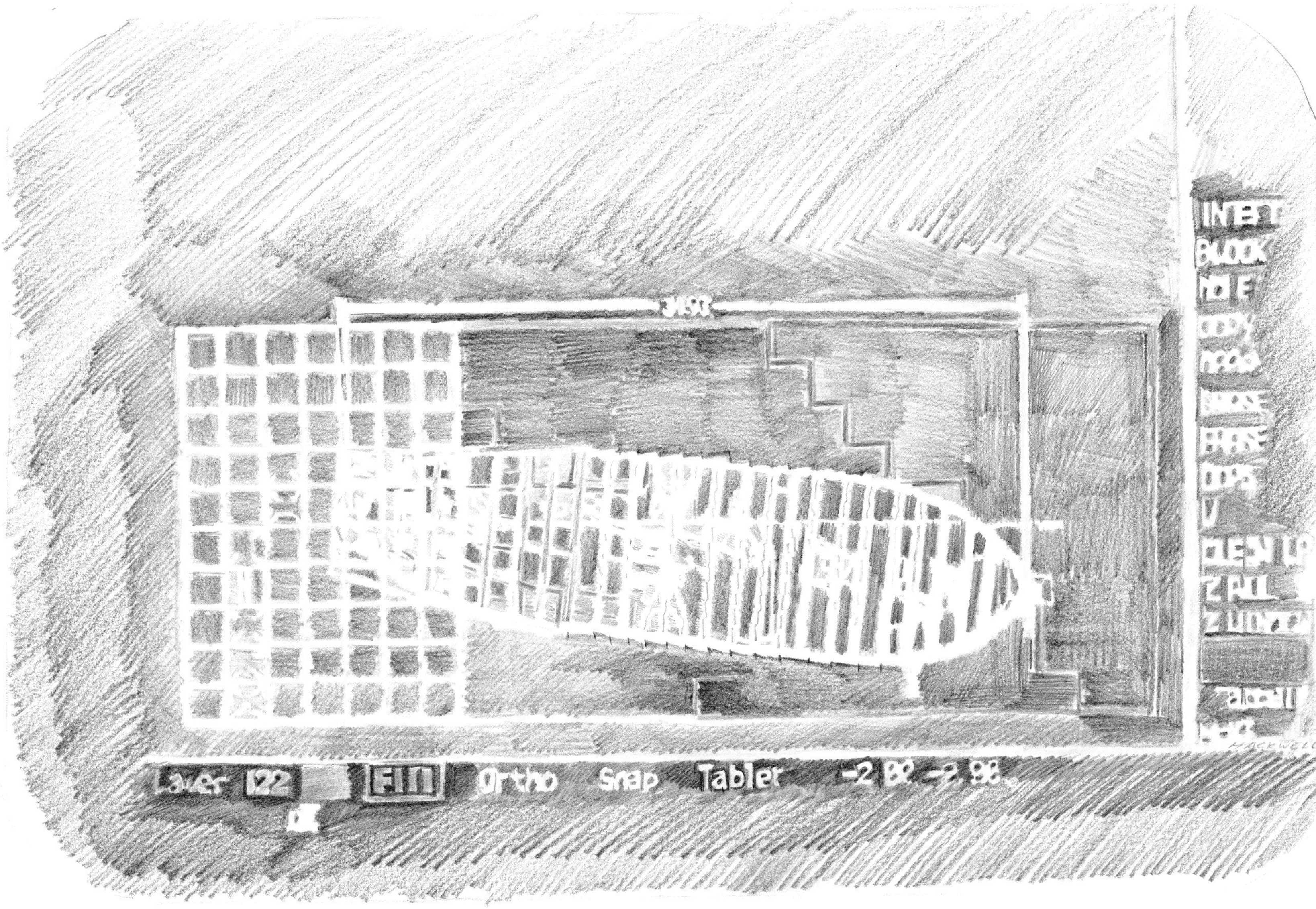
BLOCK
Ortho
Snap

debris every hour. It must be operated by two people, one to hold the dredge and another to stir the seabed by hand. The swirling sand is caught by the intake and deposited some distance from the wreck. All excess mud and sand must be kept relatively handy since most of it will be replaced over the wreck at the conclusion of the expedition, thus preserving the remains and preventing looters from gaining easy access to the treasure.

While the photographers capture pictures of each step of the project, the water dredge digs a crater around any large objects to undermine them for easy removal. At the same time a team headed by a staff archaeologist makes trial soundings by digging trenches at various points about the wreck.

The data analyst in the computer room continually updates information concerning progress at the site. As the ship's superstructure is progressively exposed, the programmer builds a three-dimensional graphic of the wreck and superimposes it over the grid positioning. Every artifact that is discovered is numbered and given a location within the individual squares. The resulting graphic is a three-dimensional picture of the shipwreck and its cargo.

Computer graphics can be enormously helpful in monitoring recovery progress. This view shows the wreck superimposed over the grid structure, with added details of artifacts thus far recovered.

Preserving Ancient Wrecks

6

● ● ● Field conservation involves the temporary cleaning and stabilization of artifacts to halt deterioration until they can be fully treated in land-based laboratories. No roles are considered more vital than those of the physical chemist, metallurgist, and biochemist who together form the conservation team on board the recovery vessel.

Removing objects from their stable underwater environment disturbs their biochemical equilibrium, and unless proper consideration is given to their vulnerability to damage, many precious objects will be lost. If certain artifacts dry out too rapidly by being suddenly exposed to sunshine or hot winds, they may even disintegrate to powder.

Raising oversized objects from the sea calls for a combination of special skills and a sense of urgency, since heavy seas could suddenly ruin a project. Here a crew positions a cannon in a safe resting place on the deck.

Huge iron cannons, for example, already corroded after some three hundred years on the seabed, will commence to rust as soon as they are exposed to the atmosphere. There may be such sudden flaking and discoloration that identifying marks—such as name and address of the manufacturer—are forever lost.

Recovering ancient wrecks is a task of recovering timber. If submerged in mud and slime, wooden hulls can survive underwater for three hundred years or more. In that time they will have been subjected to the ravages of a hostile environment. Protrusions will have been smashed by tides, and salt water grubs will have riddled the hulls full of large holes.

When suddenly exposed to the atmosphere, such timbers present the conservators with unique and unpredictable challenges. Divers attach foam padding to hull remains before winching them from the sea, since chains and heavy ropes would place too much strain on the wood.

When the timbers are brought onto the deck, the conservation team places them in large salt water or liquid wax tanks to prevent shock from hot winds that would cause them to twist or crack and fall apart. If the hull pieces are too large for the tanks, the conservator sprays them with wax preservatives to enable the water to slowly evaporate from within the wood, leaving it in a more stable condition. If the field staff can get the timber to the land-based laboratory, it will be allowed to soak for several years in a tank of polyethylene glycol until all water is diffused.

When divers bring crustacean-covered objects on deck, the conservators cannot yield to the temptation to hit them with a hammer to quickly discover what treasure they contain. If they suspect that the contents may be extremely delicate, they place the mass in a bath of sulphuric acid until an X-ray later can determine the contents more accurately.

Divers often discover a cache of coins or a stockpile of cannonballs fused together in such a way that they are impossible to handle. In this case a sledge hammer or a well-

Here a team of conservators has placed a large sheet of clear polyethylene over a piece of timber recovered from an ancient wreck while they trace the shape of the wood onto the sheet for future reference.

Here corrosion chemists use chemicals to remove crustaceans from what is believed to be a very early watch.

calculated explosive charge is permissible to break the cluster into a manageable size. On deck the physical chemist places the coins in an electrolytic bath and removes the corrosion. After several hours of polishing by the crew, silver guilders can be restored to their original luster.

Some artifacts are washed in distilled water until they are free of all salt particles, and then they are preserved with wax or lacquer. Ceramics, such as unglazed jars, are washed in diluted alcohol and then sprayed with a lacquer preservative.

As more artifacts are recovered, the conservators work closely with the archaeological team to find the artifacts most likely to provide clues to the origin or nationality of the wreck. They are also keen to discover the route the ship was on when it sank or any information about the personnel on board.

If unopened medical, pharmaceutical, or wine bottles are discovered, chemists analyze and measure the contents. This, too, may provide evidence of the wreck's origins.

Using only a pencil and calipers, archaeological artists can recreate entire artifacts when only fragments have been found.

Chinese or English plates may have been used on the captain's table moments before the ship sank. Such pieces will also bear the name and city of the maker.

Jars of salted foods and supplies of spices may provide vital data about the ship's crew. The ship's stove and cooking utensils reveal further information concerning diet and food preparation. Other artifacts, such as copper stern post fittings, may even reveal the coppersmith's name, thus providing an excellent clue as to where the ship was made.

A mass of skeletal remains found chained together would suggest that the ship was carrying prisoners, perhaps even potential mutineers, when it sank. Their position would further suggest that the captain refused them permission to dive overboard during the disaster.

Despite the academic and scientific approach being taken, all team members at this stage cannot resist the excitement of speculating about the origin and plight of the ancient wreck, knowing however, that ideas and theories will be continually modified as each fresh piece of evidence is gathered.

With the excavation complete, the research team returns to base, there to begin the long and tedious task of preserving and documenting their finds.

Cannonballs are often found in enormous quantities. Calculated explosive charges are sometimes necessary to prise them apart and make them more manageable to divers.

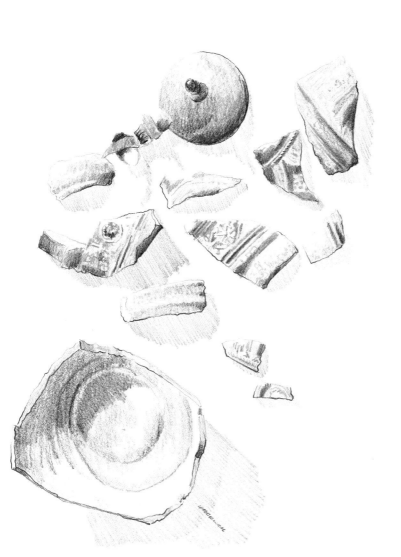

A Westerwald jug before assembly.

A Westerwald jug after assembly.

Saving the Future

● ● ● Maritime museums can be found all over the world. Here the careful and painstaking work of conservators and other scientists is brought within reach of everyone.

Creative displays of ancient wrecks and their contents, some with life-size models dressed in period costume, enable visitors to enter an ancient time capsule—to be an observer at an historic gun battle on the high seas, perhaps—and surely to share in the excitement of the recovery of the wreck itself. Such recreations ensure that mankind's maritime history is preserved for future generations to enjoy.

Marine archaeology is an important and exciting frontier. Because it is a twentieth-century science, its potential has yet to be realized. Like the oceans and waterways of the world, which themselves have no boundaries, archaeologists are the means by which all people gain a sense of interconnectedness.

Marine archaeology also brings concern for the undersea environment to international attention. Knowing only too well that pollution has severely damaged this great frontier, archaeological divers join with all the inhabitants on this earth in pleading for a balanced use of our natural riches.

By diving to the past, marine archaeology is saving the future.

INDEX